W9-DIJ-122

Thomas Paine

Political Writer

Colonial Leaders

Lord Baltimore *English Politician and Colonist*
Benjamin Banneker *American Mathematician and Astronomer*
William Bradford *Governor of Plymouth Colony*
Benjamin Franklin *American Statesman, Scientist, and Writer*
Anne Hutchinson *Religious Leader*
Cotton Mather *Author, Clergyman, and Scholar*
William Penn *Founder of Democracy*
John Smith *English Explorer and Colonist*
Miles Standish *Plymouth Colony Leader*
Peter Stuyvesant *Dutch Military Leader*

Revolutionary War Leaders

Benedict Arnold *Traitor to the Cause*
Nathan Hale *Revolutionary Hero*
Alexander Hamilton *First U.S. Secretary of the Treasury*
Patrick Henry *American Statesman and Speaker*
Thomas Jefferson *Author of the Declaration of Independence*
John Paul Jones *Father of the U.S. Navy*
Thomas Paine *Political Writer*
Paul Revere *American Patriot*
Betsy Ross *American Patriot*
George Washington *First U.S. President*

Thomas Paine

Political Writer

Bruce and Becky Durost Fish

Arthur M. Schlesinger, jr.
Senior Consulting Editor

Chelsea House Publishers

Philadelphia

Produced by 21st Century Publishing and Communications, Inc. New York, NY. http://www.21cpc.com

CHELSEA HOUSE PUBLISHERS
Editor in Chief Stephen Reginald
Production Manager Pamela Loos
Director of Photography Judy L. Hasday
Art Director Sara Davis
Managing Editor James D. Gallagher

Staff for *THOMAS PAINE*
Project Editor/Publishing Coordinator Jim McAvoy
Associate Art Director Takeshi Takahashi
Series Design Keith Trego

The Chelsea House World Wide Web address is http://www.chelseahouse.com

First Printing
1 3 5 7 9 8 6 4 2

Library of Congress Cataloging-in-Publication Data

Fish, Becky Durost.
Thomas Paine / by Becky Durost Fish and Bruce Fish.
80 pp. cm. — (Revolutionary War Leaders series)
Includes bibliographical references and index.
Summary: A biography of the writer whose pamphlet "Common Sense" helped convince American colonists to fight for their freedom.
ISBN 0-7910-5356-3 (hc)   ISBN 0-7910-5699-6 (pb)
1. Paine, Thomas, 1737-1809—Juvenile literature. 2. Political scienists—United States—Biography—Juvenile literature. 3. Revolution-aries—United States—Biography—Juvenile literature. [1. Paine, Thomas, 1737-1809. 2. Political scienists.] I. Title. II. Series.
JC178.V5F57   1999
320.5'1'092—dc21   99-20929
[B]   CIP

Contents

Tom grew up in a quiet English country village much like this one. Even though he lived far from the ocean, Tom often dreamed of being on a ship and having adventures far away at sea.

Tom's Childhood

It was a cold winter day. Suddenly an infant's cry tore through the air. The baby had just been born. He had brown hair and blue eyes. His parents named him Thomas Paine. Mr. and Mrs. Paine had been married for three years. They had never had a baby before. On January 29, 1737, that all changed.

The Paines probably sent for a **midwife** when Mrs. Paine started having her baby. A midwife was a woman who helped other women when they were giving birth. In those days, doctors did not deliver babies. All the doctors were men. People thought that only women should take care of having babies.

The new baby didn't like the cold air. His parents tried to keep him warm. They wrapped him in blankets. They kept a fire burning day and night. The warmth from the fire didn't reach very far. Cold wind blew through cracks around the door and windows. Everyone was cold during the winter. Even the king's castle was cold.

Mr. and Mrs. Paine lived in a small house in Thetford, England. Their town was 70 miles northeast of London. It was considered to be way out in the country. It took two days to travel from Thetford to London at that time. And there were not many things to do in the little village.

Tom's parents did not have much money. But they did not mind. They loved their son. They gave him everything he wanted. Sometimes they gave up things so that Tom could have something he liked. Some people thought that the Paines spoiled their boy.

One day Mrs. Paine had another baby. This time the baby was a girl. Tom was happy to have a little sister. Mr. and Mrs. Paine were glad to have another child. But the baby soon died.

Mrs. Paine never had another baby. Most of their neighbors had many children. But Mr. and Mrs. Paine just had Tom. They had already lost one child, so they did not want anything bad to happen to their only son.

In those days many children died before they were 10 years old. There were no cures for measles or **smallpox**. Many died of these or other illnesses. They had accidents, too. In bitter cold winter, some children stood too close to the big fires that kept homes warm, and their clothes caught on fire. Then they got bad burns and died.

Mr. and Mrs. Paine watched Tom all the time. They thought he was the best little boy in the world. They wanted to keep him safe.

In most of Britain, people had to pay for their children to go to school. Poor people did not have enough money for school. Their children went to work when they were very young. But Tom was lucky. In Thetford, a rich man paid for all the local children to go to school.

When Tom was six years old, he started going to school. His parents wanted him to do well. Tom learned to read and write. He liked science. He also learned about the Bible.

Tom liked his teacher, who used to work on a ship. The man told exciting stories about life at sea. Tom did not live near the sea. But he liked to dream. He dreamed of living on a big ship.

The school had a small library. Poor people did not have books. So Tom read the books in the library. One of the books told about plants and animals in the American colony of Virginia. They were very different from the plants and animals Tom saw in his own village.

Virginia was far away. It was all the way across the ocean from where Tom lived. Tom decided that one day he would travel. He would get on a ship and go to the other side of the Atlantic Ocean. He wanted to see what things really looked like in Virginia.

But Tom was too young to go on a ship. He

Young boys study and recite their lessons in a one-room village schoolhouse. Tom was a good student in most subjects, but he did not like to study Latin.

had to stay in school. He did not like some of his schoolwork. Science was fun. But Latin was no fun at all.

Tom's parents wanted him to learn to read Latin. In those days the best jobs went to men who knew Latin. Mr. and Mrs. Paine thought if Tom could read Latin, he would get a good job and have a better life. He would not be poor and live lives like theirs.

Tom was smart. He could learn Latin without difficulty. But he did not want to do things that were boring. He wanted to have fun. Latin to Tom was boring, so he didn't study it hard. His grades in Latin were very poor. This made his parents worried. They were afraid their son would never get a good job.

Tom's father worked six days a week. On Sunday the Paine family went to church. Their neighbors also went to church. Mrs. Paine belonged to the Church of England. The king was the head of this church. Most people in Britain belonged to it. Services were very formal. Bells rang at different times during the service. Candles were lit inside of the church. Tom could smell the sweet incense burning. The organ played. The services lasted a long time. Tom had to sit very still and be quiet.

Tom's father did not belong to the Church of England. He was a Quaker. Their services were simple. People sat or talked quietly. There was no music. They did not burn incense. Tom also learned about his father's church.

After church, Tom studied Bible verses. He memorized many verses. Mr. and Mrs. Paine were proud that their son knew the Bible so well.

Tom was growing quickly. Every year, his parents sent him to school. Tom did well in science and reading. But Latin was still a problem. His parents were sad. How was Tom going to get a good job if he did not learn Latin?

They talked with Tom about this. "You must do well in Latin," they said. "If you don't, you will be poor like us." No matter what his parents said, Tom did not change. He did not like Latin.

Years passed. Mr. and Mrs. Paine kept giving Tom more chances to do better in school. But Tom was very stubborn. Finally his parents made a difficult decision: if Tom was not going to learn Latin, he needed to help his family make money. They took Tom out of school. He would learn to do his father's work. Tom was not sure he liked this idea.

Tom dreamed of making his fortune on a big ship like this one. As a teenager he ran away from home and spent three years at sea.

The Runaway

Tom was 13 years old. He liked working for his father even less than he liked Latin. Mr. Paine had a small shop. He made women's corsets. In those days, women wore corsets under their dresses.

Corsets were made from fabric and pieces of whalebone. The stiff whalebone held in the ladies' waists. The whalebone also held the skirts of the dresses away from the body. The big, puffy skirts helped make women's waists look small.

Tom soon found out how hard his father really worked. Day after day Tom learned to sew corsets.

He learned to cut whalebone, measure material, and thread a needle. He also learned to smile at people and be polite to them in the shop, even when he did not want to.

Tom did not like making corsets. His back ached from bending over the workbench all day. His fingers got sore from repeatedly getting poked with sharp needles. Worst of all, it was very, very boring. Nothing changed. Every day he did the same thing.

As he stitched a seam, he would think about school. Maybe he should have worked harder. But it was too late to think about that. Tom had to work for his living.

For the next three years, Tom worked very hard and he was very unhappy. He felt trapped. He would be sewing corsets for the rest of his life. There was nothing else he could do. Or was there? Then he remembered the stories his teacher used to tell about ships. Tom began to dream about the sea. Life on a ship would be very different, he thought. Someday, he told himself, he would live on a ship and sail far out to sea. But how could that happen? He was not even near the sea.

Suddenly Tom had a great idea. He could become a sailor. That would be much better than making women's corsets for the rest of his life. The more he thought about it, the more he knew it was the right thing for him to do. Tom decided to run away.

One night, not very long thereafter, Tom crept quietly out of his home, down the path, and to the road. Then he made his way toward the ocean. When he arrived at the water's edge, he looked at all the different and magnificent ships resting in the harbor. There was one ship named *Terrible*, which seemed like a pretty good ship, despite its name. Tom decided he would work on that ship. He was going to make his fortune.

No one wondered why a 16-year-old boy wanted to work on a ship and go to sea. Lots of teenaged boys lived on their own in those days.

Tom was hired and welcomed aboard by Captain Death. Tom was going to work for a pirate.

Just before the *Terrible* set sail, Mr. Paine caught up with his son. He told Tom that it would be an awful mistake to go away with the pirate. Mr. Paine gave many reasons for Tom to go back home. His mother needed him badly. The shop needed him to get the work done. And also, sometimes ships sank and all of their crews drowned at sea. Finally Tom agreed to go back home.

But he was not happy. He hated making corsets. His mother nagged him all the time. Nothing he did seemed to please her. She was always finding something to complain about. His mother could never forgive him for not learning Latin.

Pirates attacked ships and stole their cargo. It was exciting for them to fight with the other crews and capture the ships. But pirates also got bored. They sometimes spent weeks looking for ships and seeing nothing but sea and sky. Some pirates were women. Mary Read and Anne Bonney were pirates who dressed themselves as men to fool the others and get on ships. In 1720 they got caught and were put in jail.

Tom read newspapers to find out about the world. He read every story about the *Terrible*. The ship was doing well. It won battles with other ships. Tom wished he had gone with the *Terrible*. Life on a ship sounded much more fun than staying at home. Anything sounded better than living with his mother and her complaints.

It was not very long before Tom ran away from home again. This time his father could not find him. Tom had signed up and sailed out to sea on the *King of Prussia*. Later, however, he never talked about his life on the ship. But after three years, Tom had had enough of the sea. He was tired of eating hard biscuits. And he did not like sailing through storms. It could

When Thomas Paine lived, ships did not have engines. They had sails. The winds blew against the ship's sails, making the ship move. The ship, being pushed only by the wind, usually took 24 hours to move only 60 miles. Sometimes the wind stopped blowing completely. Then a ship would not move at all. It could sit motionless for days and days, going nowhere. Also, big and powerful storms at sea might damage or even destroy a ship.

be very cold, wet, and miserable.

Tom came back to Britain. He was 20 years old then. He knew that he did not want to live with his parents again. So he settled in the big city of London. There were many interesting and exciting things in London. But first Tom needed a job. There was only one thing he knew how to do—make corsets. So he opened a shop and began to make corsets.

Over the next few years, Tom moved from town to town, never quite feeling settled. In one town he met a girl named Mary. She worked as a maid. Tom and Mary began seeing each other and fell in love. Soon they were married.

But Tom and Mary were not happy for long. Tom owed a lot of money. He could have been arrested for this. At the time in Britain, if somebody owed others money and could not pay the debts, that person would be put in jail. One night Tom and Mary ran away from the town they lived in. They did not want Tom to land in jail. Less than a year later, Mary fell ill and died.

The skyline of bustling 18th-century London, where Tom first lived and worked after giving up his life at sea.

Tom was very sad. His business had failed. His wife had died. He was all alone and broke. During the next few years, Tom drifted from job to job. Sometimes he taught. Sometimes he collected taxes for the government. He was not very good at any of his jobs.

But Tom made friends easily. And he loved hearing about and discussing the news. After work, Tom often got together with his friends. They would debate events in the news. Usually Tom won.

Tom's friends liked him. They knew he was not perfect, but he was a nice guy. Tom was not especially good-looking. He had a large nose and his skin was covered with scars. But Tom thought women fell in love with him as soon as they saw him. His friends did not agree. They thought Tom was **vain**.

When he was 34 years old, Tom married again. He was collecting taxes at the time, but he was still poor. Other people who collected taxes for the government were also poor. Tom thought that the government was not paying them enough. It was not fair. He and his friends worked hard to get money for the government.

They should be paid more money for their work. He tried to get a pay raise for everyone who collected taxes.

Tom wrote out the reasons why tax collectors should be paid more. The article was printed and Tom handed out hundreds of copies. Even people who didn't agree with him liked the way he wrote.

Tom worked very hard but did not get the pay raise. One good thing did happen during this time. Tom met a man named Benjamin Franklin. Mr. Franklin liked Tom. He wished more people would work to make things fair like Tom did.

Mr. Franklin was from America. America was not a country yet. In America there were 13 **colonies** that were ruled by Great Britain. There were quarrels between Britain and the American colonies. The king of Britain wanted more control of the colonies. He also wanted to tax the colonies more. The colonists did not like the way they were being treated by the king, and

**Benjamin Franklin met Tom in London.
He liked Tom and encouraged him to
start a new life in America.**

they wanted more freedom from Britain.

Benjamin Franklin came to London as the
spokesman for the American colonies. He

wanted the king to treat the American colonies fairly.

A couple of years later, Tom was in trouble. He was not getting along with his wife. They agreed to live apart. Then Tom lost his job again.

Mr. Franklin heard what had happened to Tom. He told Tom to leave Britain. He said Tom could have a better life in America.

Mr. Franklin wrote letters to people he knew in America. The letters asked people to help Tom start a new life. With these letters Tom's dream was about to come true. He would see America for himself. In October 1774 Tom got on a ship and headed for the distant land called America.

Benjamin Franklin was one of the best-known men in colonial America. From 1757 to 1775, he spent most of his time living in London, serving as an agent for the American colonies.

When the armed conflicts began between the American colonies and Britain, Franklin was very upset. He stated, "I would try anything and bear anything that can be borne with safety to our just liberties, rather than engage in a war . . ." In 1775, when it was clear to everyone that there was no hope for peace, Franklin left London with tears in his eyes and a deep sadness in his heart.

The harbor in Philadelphia was a very busy place in 1774 when Tom arrived. He was treated very well by many people there because he carried letters of introduction from Benjamin Franklin, who was highly respected.

3

Getting Ready for War

Tom decided that he would arrive in America in style. He didn't want to be one of the passengers stuck down in the **hold** of the ship. It was a damp, smelly place. Many people got sick there. Some even died.

Tom had some money from his wife. He used it to buy a first-class ticket on a ship. He stayed in a nice cabin instead of the smelly hold.

It did not make much difference in the end. Sickness swept through the entire ship. Tom became very sick. He was so sick, he thought he was going to die.

When Tom got sick on the ship and later in prison, he probably got a disease called typhus. Typhus spreads by body lice going from one person to another. It was common in crowded places like ships and prisons. The disease gives a person headaches, chills, fever, and body aches. It took months for Tom to get better. Many people died from getting typhus.

A few weeks later the ship landed in America. It docked at the harbor in Philadelphia, Pennsylvania. But Tom was still quite sick. He was terribly weak. He could not even roll over in bed without help.

A doctor checked all the passengers on the ship. When he got to Tom, he discovered the letters from Benjamin Franklin. Mr. Franklin was well-known and very popular throughout Philadelphia.

Because of the letters from Mr. Franklin, the doctor believed that Tom was an important man. He hired men to carry Tom off the ship and found a good place for him to stay and rest. The doctor made sure Tom got the best care possible.

In spite of this very special care, Tom was

sick for another six weeks. As soon as he got better, he wrote an article. The article was printed in a local newspaper. Tom liked seeing his words in print. He decided to look for a job in writing. Soon he was hired to write for a new magazine called *Pennsylvania Magazine.* People liked to read Tom's articles and that helped the magazine sell well. About 1,500 copies of each issue were sold, and Tom had articles in all of them.

Tom liked his job very much. For once, he was not bored working. People came into the office and argued about King George III of Britain. They were angry with Britain. New taxes and laws that were passed in Britain made life harder in America. Many people thought the king did not understand how hard they worked and what their lives were really like. Tom had always liked debates. He enjoyed hearing both sides of this debate.

Then in April, shocking news reached Philadelphia. British troops had shot at men

The Boston Massacre, in which British troops fired on a group of ordinary townspeople. This terrible event inspired Tom to try to help the cause of freedom in the colonies.

near Boston. Some of the men had been killed. Tom could not believe it. He was not enjoying the debates anymore. He was very angry. It was not fair for the king's armed soldiers to shoot at ordinary citizens. Tom wanted to do something to help the cause.

Beginning early in April 1775, Tom began to fight in the only way he knew. He started writing. He wrote one article after another. Each article argued that the British were wrong. Many people began agreeing with Tom.

Tom was also upset by something else that was very unfair. People were buying and selling slaves. A slave market stood right across the street from Tom's home. So Tom decided that he would write against slavery as well. He blamed Britain for the slavery.

The slave trade was a thriving and major British industry for more than 100 years before the American Revolution. Over time, an estimated 2 million slaves were transported to British colonies. It was common to see advertising selling slaves. Tom was very concerned and his thoughtful writing on the issues around slavery had a big impact on Thomas Jefferson. In fact, in the original Declaration of Independence, Jefferson went so far as to place the blame for the slave trade on Britain's King George III. This part of the Declaration was totally cut out because some powerful people did not agree with it.

Tom thought people in the colonies might end up fighting the British. The colonists got all their goods and supplies from Britain. But if they fought the British, they would not be able to get those supplies anymore. That gave Tom an idea. Tom knew the colonists would need gunpowder.

Tom had always liked science. He started doing some **experiments**. Then he came up with a way for families to be able to make some of the materials that went into gunpowder. He thought it would help the colonists win a war against Britain.

In May Benjamin Franklin returned to Philadelphia. Leaders from the other colonies came to the city too. These leaders held many meetings. They were all very concerned and tried to decide what to do about the fighting in Boston. They voted and agreed to make George Washington a general and put him in charge of the soon-to-be-formed Colonial Army. But they could not agree on much else.

While they met, Tom listened to people talking. He considered everyone's ideas. That fall he wrote an article. Tom said that the colonies should become a separate nation from Britain.

Many people were shocked when they read this. They did not know that their leaders agreed with Tom. The leaders had been careful not to say anything like this in public. Publicly they kept talking about solving the problems with King George of Britain. The leaders knew that the people did not want to think about breaking away from Britain. But Tom was not afraid to write what he thought.

People started to pay attention to what Tom wrote. His articles were different. Most writers used big words that were hard to understand. But Tom had not gone to college. He wrote the way most people talked. He understood how ordinary people felt.

The colonists did not know what to do about their problems with Britain. Most of them did not want to go to war. Laws from Britain caused some difficulties. Other than that, life was pretty good. They knew that war would be hard and people would die. Britain was very strong and had a powerful army. The colonists might lose the war. Then King George would punish them.

Later that fall, Tom and some of his friends decided that the people needed to hear all the good reasons for fighting against Britain. They had many long discussions. Tom wrote the ideas down and revised them for many months, until the words were just right.

Finally his writing was finished, and Tom had it published. His new work was called *Common Sense*. In this 47-page **pamphlet**, Tom explained why having a king was bad. He told people why their lives would be better without Britain. He talked about their dreams.

In the pamphlet, Tom went on to say: "A government of our own is a natural right." And **Patriots** were overjoyed to read these words: "The sun never shined on a cause more just." Tom believed that the cause of America was

COMMON SENSE;

ADDRESSED TO THE

INHABITANTS

O F

A M E R I C A,

On the following interesting

S U B J E C T S.

I. Of the Origin and Design of Government in general,
with concise Remarks on the English Constitution.

II. Of Monarchy and Hereditary Succession.

III. Thoughts on the present State of American Affairs.

IV. Of the present Ability of America, with some miscellaneous Reflections.

Man knows no Master save creating HEAVEN,
Or those whom choice and common good ordain.
THOMSON.

PHILADELPHIA;
Printed, and Sold, by R. BELL, in Third-Street.
MDCC LXX VI.

In Tom's pamphlet, *Common Sense*, he encouraged the American colonists to break away from British rule.

that of all mankind. On the last page of *Common Sense* Tom wrote clearly and firmly: "The Free and independent States of America."

Common Sense was printed in January 1776. On the same day that *Common Sense* went on sale, something important arrived in a ship. It was a copy of King George's latest speech. The king said that the protests in the colonies must be stopped.

People read what the king said. They read what Tom said. Thousands and thousands of people bought *Common Sense.* In the first three months, 120,000 copies of *Common Sense* were sold. Altogether sales reached half a million. Because there were so few people then, it would be like selling more than 15 million copies in America today.

For the first time, ordinary people in the colonies started thinking that they did not need the king anymore. Tom's writing convinced them that they should fight for freedom. His words had an especially strong impact on young and idealistic people. Soon many young men joined the militia and were ready to fight for liberty and go to war against Britain.

Tom made some money from selling *Common Sense.* But he would not take any of the money for himself. He asked some friends to use the money to buy mittens for colonial soldiers. The soldiers were fighting in Canada during a cold winter. Tom wanted to help them get warm.

That spring the colonial leaders stayed in Philadelphia. They debated whether to make a country separate from Britain. By June the decision was made. Thomas Jefferson began to write the Declaration of Independence.

On July 4, 1776, the leaders approved the Declaration of Independence. The war for freedom began. Most ordinary people in the colonies agreed with their leaders. What Tom had written helped to make people ready for the war. *Common Sense* changed people's minds.

General George Washington and his troops faced a terrible winter in 1776–77. After reading Tom's article, "The American Crisis," many soldiers decided to continue fighting.

4

The Revolutionary War

Tom was worried. He was with General George Washington and the colonial troops. It was December 1776. The war was not going well.

Winter had set in, and it was very cold. The soldiers were living outside in tents. Snow kept falling. Some soldiers did not have boots, and some did not even have shoes. They wrapped their feet in rags. Many of them got sick.

There was not enough food, either. The men were tired, cold, sick, and very unhappy. They missed their families. They were ready to give up. Some of them left the army. They went home where at least it was warm.

The British army kept coming. The colonists kept pulling back. The British army marched through New Jersey. They were now just across the river from Philadelphia. Everyone was very scared. If the British attacked Philadelphia, they might win. The colonies would be split into two parts. Then the whole war might be lost.

Tom did not want the colonies to lose the war. If that happened, the United States would not be free. The king of Britain would punish the Americans for fighting him. People like General Washington and Tom would be arrested because they were leaders. They might even be killed.

Some officers came to Tom. They told him he needed to leave the army. He could help the new country most by going to Philadelphia. There he could write something. They hoped Tom could get people excited about freedom again. If he failed, the war for freedom might fail too.

Tom went back to Philadelphia. He listened to the people's discussions there. They were angry because the Colonial Army was pulling back. Tom knew this was a real crisis, and he had to do something about it. He sat down and wrote out his thoughts. His article, called "The American Crisis," was published in the *Pennsylvania Magazine* on December 19, 1776.

"These are the times that try men's souls," Tom wrote. He praised all the soldiers who would stand and fight for freedom. He said they deserved "the love and thanks of man and woman." His article continued, "The harder the conflict, the more glorious the triumph."

Some say that Tom wrote "The American Crisis" on a drumhead beside an army campfire while he was with Washington's army, retreating through New Jersey. His words urged people to keep fighting under very difficult conditions.

Just a few days after Tom's article was published, on December 26, 1776, General Washington led the army to victory over the British at Trenton.

Tom wrote 18 important articles during the war to help and encourage Americans in their fight for independence.

General George Washington liked Tom's words. He ordered all the soldiers to read them. Most soldiers decided to stay and fight. They would not give up. Once again, Tom's words made the difference.

But the war was far from over. It would drag on for three more years. Sometimes it looked like Britain would win. Sometimes it seemed as though America would win.

One thing was clear: the American soldiers needed pay and supplies. They did not have enough guns, ammunition, or clothing. And they did not get paid, so they could not send money home to their families.

Tom was working for Pennsylvania's government at the time. He saw the problems the soldiers were having. He decided to do something to help. First he gave $500 of his own money to help pay the soldiers. Then he asked his rich friends to do the same thing.

The rich people wanted to win the war too. They knew that if they lost the war, they would

A drawing of Tom. His words always inspired colonial Americans to keep working toward freedom.

lose all their money. So they gave a lot of money for the soldiers. The money that was collected was put in a bank. It was the first bank to be started in America and was called the Bank of Pennsylvania.

Tom also saw that the separate colonies were not getting along. He feared that their disagreements would cause them to lose sight of what they were fighting for. If they started fighting against each other instead of Britain, they might lose the war. He sat down and wrote *Public Good.* In this pamphlet Tom asked the colonies to work together for the good of the whole nation.

> "Our citizenship in the United States is our national character. Our citizenship in any particular State is only our local distinction. By the latter we are known at home, by the former to the world. Our great title is AMERICANS."
>
> *Thomas Paine*

In spite of all his work, the army still needed more supplies. The American leaders decided to send some men to France to ask for help. King Louis XVI of France did not like King George of Britain. The French and English had been fighting each other for years. The Americans hoped that the king of France would help America fight against Britain.

Benjamin Franklin drew this cartoon showing the colonies as parts of a snake. He was trying to encourage Americans to work together as a single unit to successfully fight the British.

A man named John Laurens was chosen to go to France. He asked that Tom go with him. Tom agreed. Some people in Philadelphia did not like Tom because he had accused one of their friends of stealing money from the government. Tom wanted to get away from Philadelphia and meet new people.

In January 1781 Tom left for France. He was scared. The last time he had been on a ship, he had gotten sick. This ship was not very strong. Parts of it were broken. What would happen this time?

At first everything went well. Then one night Tom felt a big shudder go through the ship. He ran up to the **deck**. The ship was surrounded by huge chunks of ice. The ice pounded against the sides of the ship. Would the ship fall apart?

Suddenly the wind started blowing, harder and harder. The ship rocked from side to side. Ice crashed against the deck. Some of the deck ripped away. Everyone was scared. The captain told his crew what to do. They all worked hard. After eight long hours, they finally made their way through all the ice. The ship was damaged, but it was still in one piece.

After three weeks at sea, Tom and the others saw land. It surely felt good to leave the rocking boat and stand on solid ground. People were waiting to greet John Laurens and Tom. The

Frenchmen surprised Tom by telling him that he was famous in France. Many people there had read Tom's writings. They thought he was a good writer and they agreed with what he said.

However, Tom was filthy. He had spent three weeks wearing the same clothes on a smelly ship. He did not even notice how bad he looked. He was used to the awful smell. Tom's only thoughts were of the job he had to do.

He traveled to Paris and met the mayor. After the meeting, Tom stayed with Mr. Watson, an American who was living in Paris. Mr. Watson knew something had to be done about his filthy guest. He offered Tom a bath. Tom said no. Finally Mr. Watson told Tom that if he took a bath, Mr. Watson would give him some newspapers from Britain to read.

Tom liked reading newspapers. So he agreed to take the bath. Mr. Watson gave Tom clean clothes and a stack of newspapers. Everyone was much happier.

Tom kept busy. He wrote reports for John

A ship in rough seas. Tom always hated traveling across the ocean because many of his trips were terrible experiences.

Laurens to send back to America. Mr. Laurens met with many French officials. After several months, John and Tom were ready to go back to America with money, clothing, and guns for the soldiers. But Tom wanted to stay in France. He did not want to go back to the place where many people did not like him. And he especially hated traveling on ships.

But John Laurens convinced Tom to leave France. The trip across the ocean was terrible. It took 86 days. They faced many storms. Tom felt sick. He thought they would never reach land.

Finally they did reach America. They sent the much-needed supplies to General Washington as quickly as they could. The assistance from the French made the difference.

In the last major battle, with fresh ammunition,

John Laurens was General George Washington's aide during the war. He was with Washington at Valley Forge during the bitter cold winter of 1777. He was also at Washington's side when, in 1781, British General Cornwallis's letter to Washington asking for a cease-fire arrived. After the surrender of the British troops, Laurens helped Washington write the report of the event to the Continental Congress.

General Washington defeated the British at Yorktown. America finally won the war and became an independent nation. People held parades and celebrations and were very happy.

Tom was one of the few people who was not happy. He did not have a job or any money. What was he going to do?

A portrait of Tom after the Revolutionary War.
He tried to avoid international politics, but his
passionate writing got him in trouble in both
England and France.

Danger
in France

The fighting was over. Tom was glad that his writing had helped win the war. But he had never taken money from selling his articles. He thought it was more important to sell the pamphlets for a low price. That way more people could read them.

At this time everyone was going back to their homes. But Tom did not have a home. He had rented the places where he lived. And he did not have any money. George Washington wanted the Continental Congress to give money to Tom. He thought it would be a good way to thank Tom for his hard work.

But Congress put off making a decision about Tom. The new nation had not paid the thousands of soldiers who had fought in the war. America owed money to other countries as well.

Some people were still mad at Tom because he accused their friend of stealing money from the government. These people were now in the Congress and they did not want to give Tom any money.

But Tom and General Washington got along well. One time while Tom was visiting General Washington, someone stole Tom's coat. George Washington gave Tom one of his own coats. Tom thought that coat was very special because General Washington had worn it. Tom wore the coat for many years after that.

General Washington and some of his friends kept working to get some money for Tom. Finally the state of Pennsylvania gave Tom some money. They knew Tom had helped make the Bank of Pennsylvania.

The state of New York also decided to help

Tom. They gave him a farm. Then the Congress decided to give Tom some money too. They voted to give Tom $3,000. Tom took the money, but he thought he should have been paid much more.

He decided he was through with politics. He wanted to study science again. Tom tried to invent a candle that would not make smoke. He showed his friend, Benjamin Franklin, some early samples of his new candle.

Tom also wanted to build an iron bridge that would not need **piers**. Most bridges were built of wood or stone. They needed piers to hold them up in the middle of a river. But in the northern parts of America, rivers froze during the winter. By early spring huge chunks of ice began floating down the rivers. The ice slammed against the piers. After a while the piers broke.

Tom thought America needed a new kind of bridge. He would make a bridge from iron. It would cross the river in a single arch.

One day Tom looked closely at a spiderweb. He noticed the web was made in sections. Webs were very strong. Tom thought that a bridge made of sections would be strong too. Like a spiderweb, it could be supported on two sides.

People in Philadelphia thought Tom's bridge was a good idea. But they were not sure that it would work. Benjamin Franklin told Tom to go to France and Britain. If Tom got experts in those countries to like his plans, then people in America might build the bridge too. So Tom set off for France.

Before Tom left, Mr. Franklin gave him some letters to take with him. They were written to Mr. Franklin's friends in France. He asked his friends to take care of Tom. Others also gave Tom letters to take to people in France.

He did not look forward to getting on a ship again. Every time Tom sailed across the ocean, bad things happened. But this time was different. They had good weather and the water was smooth. Tom had a good time.

Just as when he arrived in America, Tom arrived in France on the eve of a **revolution**–in

Many modern bridges owe their design to Tom's idea. He imagined an iron bridge suspended from above by cables that were attached to towers on either side of a river.

May 1787. He was welcomed as a hero. France was having problems, and the French people were very angry with King Louis XVI.

Mr. Franklin's friends liked Tom. Tom also met Thomas Jefferson in Paris and got along well with him. Tom did not pay much attention to politics there. He was working on his bridge.

After three months the French experts said that Tom's bridge was a good idea. He left the next day for Britain. In Britain there were some people who wanted to change their government, so they gave Tom an equally warm welcome.

Over the next several years, Tom went back and forth between Britain and France. People in France were getting ready to bring down the king. Tom thought that the people in France were not being treated fairly by King Louis. But he did not get involved. He wanted to see his bridge built.

Then in October 1789, thousands of French women got very angry. Flour was scarce. A single loaf of bread cost almost as much as what their husbands earned in a full workday. The women feared their families would starve to death. The king was not doing anything about it.

The women marched to the palace and demanded action. They ran through the palace rooms and made lots of noise. The king and queen were scared. King Louis agreed to do something.

Tom heard about this while he was in Britain and got excited. "A share in two revolutions," he said, "is living to some purpose."

Then a famous Englishman named Edmund Burke, who had supported America during the war, wrote a book defending the French king. Mr. Burke said changing the government was bad. He thought the rights of normal people did not matter.

Tom knew Mr. Burke was all wrong. He wrote a book to answer Mr. Burke. It was called *The Rights of Man*. Tom had always fought for fairness. He thought kings often treated their people badly. This was not right. He wrote that ordinary people had certain rights. Kings needed to

The Rights of Man sold two million copies in England, France, and America. In it Tom called on Englishmen to join France and the United States in a government "of the people and for the people and by the people."

Part Two of *The Rights of Man* was published in 1792. It almost pushed Britain to the edge of revolution. The British government became very angry at Tom for this. In London and many other cities in Britain people burned dummies in Tom's likeness to show their great displeasure.

change the way they dealt with the common man.

Some people in Britain did not like what Tom wrote. They called it **treason** against the king of Britain. They went to arrest Tom. The American **ambassador** told Tom to flee, saying that his American citizenship would not protect him. So Tom escaped. He got on a ship and headed for France, where he once again was welcomed as a hero. Then Tom was elected a member of the revolutionary French Assembly.

The English courts ruled that Tom was guilty of treason against the king. They said that his book could not be sold in Britain. If Tom returned to Britain, he would be thrown in jail.

Tom was too busy in France to worry about being an outlaw in Britain. King Louis no longer ruled. He was a prisoner. The new French leaders were making a new government that would give ordinary people more rights. Tom liked these changes, but he did not like one thing: some of the new leaders wanted to kill the king and all his supporters.

King Louis XVI of France is captured by revolutionaries. Later, both the king and queen were executed.

Tom thought the king should not be killed. He said the king should be sent to live in America. But some of the new French leaders hated the king very much. They were led by a man named Mr. Robespierre. He controlled the new government, and he ordered the king and queen of France to be killed.

Soon the **radical** leaders started arresting anyone who disagreed with them. Many of Tom's friends were arrested and killed. Tom became unpopular with the French radicals.

Tom was afraid. He knew that the radicals did not like him. They thought he had been wrong to try to save the king's life. He might be the next person to be arrested. What should he do?

Tom could not leave France. The English were stopping all boats to see if he was on them. If he tried to get away, the English would catch him and put him in jail.

Tom decided to stay in Paris. But he tried to help his friends escape. Some of his friends got away. Some were arrested.

With so many of his friends getting arrested and killed, Tom did not think he would live for long. He had always wanted to write a book about God and the church. Tom thought he was running out of time, so he sat down and began writing what he thought to be his final work.

One night he heard banging on the gates at the house where he lived. Soldiers came in. Tom was sure he was going to be arrested. But he was not. The soldiers were after two of Tom's friends. Those friends had escaped just two days before.

A month later the soldiers came knocking again. This time they arrested Tom's landlord. Tom knew he did not have much time left. He worked hard to finish his book. The next day he did. He called his book *The Age of Reason.*

Tom went out that night with friends to celebrate. Then he went to bed. At four o'clock in the morning, someone banged on his door. Tom stumbled out of bed and opened the door. Five policemen stood there. They arrested him. It was December 28, 1793.

He wondered what would happen next. Would he be in prison for very long? Or was he about to be killed, like so many of his friends?

Many bloody battles took place during the
French Revolution. After being arrested because
of his political views, Tom spent a terrifying
year in a French prison and nearly died there.

Dark Days in Prison

At first Tom wrote many letters after his arrest. He wanted every friend he could think of to know that he was in prison. He hoped that Thomas Jefferson or some other people in America might help to get him freed.

The French kept Tom in prison. As the weeks turned into months, Tom wondered what was going to happen. He had not been taken to court for a trial. But he had not been set free either.

Things got worse. In March 1794 Tom was told that no one could send messages from the prison any longer. Letters sent to Tom were not delivered either. For six months Tom did not hear any news from outside except from the guards.

He found old friends in the prison. But everyday some of his friends were taken away. Their heads were cut off. He became convinced that he was going to be killed soon.

Tom knew he could not do anything to save himself. So he tried to help the others in prison with him. He listened to their problems. He joked with them. He talked to them and gave them things to think about so they would not worry about being killed.

Tom also kept writing. He went over his book, *The Age of Reason*, and changed some of the words. The book was smuggled out of prison so that other people could read it.

In the middle of June the Great Terror began. The leaders of France said that people charged with crimes could not have lawyers and could not call witnesses. If a judge found someone guilty, the person was sentenced to die. Hundreds of people in the prison started being killed at the

guillotine. This was a French invention that cut people's heads off. As many as 400 people were killed in one day in Paris alone.

Tom had been in prison for six months by this time. Every night when he went to sleep, he was certain that he would be killed the next day. It was hard for Tom to live like that. Near the end of June he got very sick. He had a high fever. He was so sick that he did not know what was going on around him. Two other prisoners took care of him. Fortunately for Tom, one of them was a doctor.

While he was so sick, even more people were killed. Finally the French people decided to take action. A group of them captured Robespierre, the leader of the radicals, and killed him. They put new people in charge. Messages could

The French prison that Tom was in was nothing like today's prisons. Prisoners did not get clothing or food. They had to pay for everything they needed. They even had to buy the wood for fires to warm themselves. Jailers did not have to get a doctor when prisoners got sick. Tom was lucky because one of his fellow prisoners was a doctor. Many people died in prison.

again be sent from the prison.

After this Tom had hope. He started to feel better. Maybe he would be freed from prison. Again he sent messages to everyone he could think of, but nothing happened.

Many of Tom's friends who had survived the Great Terror had been set free. However, Tom still stayed in prison. Some of his old enemies were still in power and they wanted to keep him locked up.

Tom learned that James Monroe was in Paris. Mr. Monroe represented the United States. Tom wrote to Mr. Monroe, asking for his help. Again nothing happened.

Tom was now one of the oldest people in the prison. He had completely run out of money. While other prisoners got food and clothing from their families, Tom had no one. He had to beg for candles, food, and soap. He got a bad sore on his side. It did not get better. After a while, the sore got much worse. He thought for sure he would die now.

James Monroe worked to get Tom set free from prison. Monroe then let Tom stay at his house in Paris for two years.

In October, Tom finally got good news. James Monroe was fighting for Tom's freedom. After weeks of discussions, the French finally agreed to set their prisoner free. Monroe went directly to the prison to get Tom. It was November 4, 1794.

Tom had been in prison for almost one year.

Monroe asked Tom to stay at his house in Paris. Tom accepted. He stayed for more than two years. It was a long time to be a guest at someone's home. Tom did not stop to think that he might be staying longer than he should have. He did not leave Monroe's home in Paris until Monroe himself had to leave France and go back to America.

James Monroe fought the war with General George Washington and was wounded in the battle at Trenton. General Washington said that Monroe was "a brave, active, and sensible officer."

Monroe became governor of Virginia and a senator in Congress. He was in France from 1790 to 1796 as United States minister. In 1817 he became the fifth president of the United States of America.

Tom moved to another place and stayed in Paris until 1802. He did not want to take a ship to America. The British often stopped ships at sea. They would take people prisoner. Tom knew some people in Britain still wanted to catch him and put him in prison. He thought he would be safer in France. Tom had seen enough of prison. He did not want to go back there ever again.

Thomas Jefferson had been elected the third president of the United States in 1801. He remembered his friend Thomas Paine. He sent a warship to France. The ship would take Tom back to the United States safely. In October 1802 Tom arrived in the city of Washington.

Tom's book, *The Age of Reason*, had been published in America while he was in France. Many people did not like what Tom said about God and the church. They thought he did not believe in God.

Even though Tom did not agree with the French radicals, many Americans still blamed him for what happened in France. People started to turn away from his books and his ideas. It became unpopular to even speak his name.

Some said that Tom began to drink too much beer and wine. They decided that he was not a good person.

More than 20 years had gone by since America's difficult war for freedom from

A portrait of Tom commemorating his written works and his contribution to the American cause of freedom.

Britain. George Washington and Benjamin Franklin were dead, so most people did not remember what Tom had done to help them win that war.

Newspapers attacked Tom. Very few people stood up for him. Some places even refused to let him rent rooms to live in.

The city of Washington was not very big. At that time cows grazed in the middle of the city. There were muddy areas full of mosquitoes. It was much different from the big city of Paris. Tom knew he was not liked by many people in Washington, so he decided to leave. He traveled to Philadelphia. He thought his old friends would welcome him there.

Some of his friends had died. Others simply would not speak to him. Tom did not stay in Philadelphia for very long. Soon he was on his way to New York City.

Tom spent the rest of his life around New York. He visited the farm he had been given at the end of the Revolutionary War. He wrote articles. But many people just ignored him. This was hard for Tom to understand. Why was he being treated like this?

In time he became sick. Sometimes he drank

a lot of brandy to cloud his mind. This made him feel even worse. On June 8, 1809, Tom died. He was 73 years old. Very few people showed up for Tom's funeral.

But that is not the end of the story. Tom's words lived on. Tom is now seen as one of the great political writers of his day. He is remembered as one of America's Revolutionary War leaders. He led people with his words. His articles, pamphlets, and books helped America become a free country. Today people still use Tom's words in their fight for freedom.

GLOSSARY

ambassador–a high-ranking official who lives in a foreign country as the representative of his or her own government

colony–a place where people live but are ruled by the laws of a faraway country

deck–the platform that goes from one side of a ship to the other

experiment–a test to prove whether an idea is correct

guillotine–a machine with a heavy blade used to cut off people's heads

hold–the inside of a ship below the deck

midwife–a woman who is trained to help other women give birth

pamphlet–a thin booklet with a paper cover

Patriots–people who believed America should be a country separate from Britain

pier–a pillar that supports a bridge

radical–a person who works for extreme changes in government

revolution–the overthrow or renouncing of a government

smallpox–a highly contagious disease that causes sores on the skin and leaves scars

treason–a plan to overthrow the government

vain–having too much pride in one's looks or abilities

CHRONOLOGY

1737 Born Thomas Paine on January 29 in Thetford, England.

1743 Begins school.

1750 Leaves school to work in his father's shop.

1753 Runs away from home to work on a pirate ship.

1757 Leaves life at sea to live and work in London.

1760s Marries first wife, Mary; wife dies.

1771 Marries second wife; works as tax collector; meets Benjamin Franklin.

1774 Separates from second wife; loses job; sails to America; arrives in Philadelphia; works as a journalist.

1776 Publishes *Common Sense* in January; publishes "American Crisis" on December 19.

1781 Makes his first trip to France; returns to America; General Washington wins the Battle of Yorktown.

1787 Sails for France.

1789 French Revolution takes place.

1791 Publishes part one of *The Rights of Man* (the second part is published in 1792).

1793 Finishes *The Age of Reason*; is arrested and put in jail in France.

1794 Freed from prison; lives with James Monroe in Paris.

1802 Returns to America.

1809 Dies on June 8 in New York City.

REVOLUTIONARY WAR TIME LINE

1765 The Stamp Act is passed by the British. Violent protests against it break out in the colonies.

1766 Britain ends the Stamp Act.

1767 Britain passes a law that taxes glass, painter's lead, paper, and tea in the colonies.

1770 Five colonists are killed by British soldiers in the Boston Massacre.

1773 People are angry about the taxes on tea. They throw boxes of tea from ships in Boston harbor into the water. It ruins the tea. The event is called the Boston Tea Party.

1774 The British pass laws to punish Boston for the Boston Tea Party. They close Boston harbor. Leaders in the colonies meet to plan a response to these actions.

1775 The battles of Lexington and Concord begin the American Revolution.

1776 The Declaration of Independence is signed. France and Spain give money to help the Americans fight Britain. Nathan Hale is captured by the British. He is charged with being a spy and is executed.

1777 Leaders choose a flag for America. The American troops win some important battles over the British. General Washington and his troops spend a very cold, hungry winter in Valley Forge.

1778 France sends ships to help the Americans win the war. The British are forced to leave Philadelphia.

1779 French ships head back to France. The French support the Americans in other ways.

1780 Americans discover that Benedict Arnold is a traitor. He escapes to the British. Major battles take place in North and South Carolina.

1781 The British surrender at Yorktown.

1783 A peace treaty is signed in France. British troops leave New York.

1787 The U.S. Constitution is written. Delaware becomes the first state in the Union.

1789 George Washington becomes the first president. John Adams is vice president.

FURTHER READING

Bangs, Edward. *Yankee Doodle.* New York: Aladdin Paperbacks, 1994.

Dalgliesh, Alice. *The Fourth of July Story.* New York: Aladdin Paperbacks, 1995.

Fisher, Leonard Everett. *Stars and Stripes: Our National Flag.* New York: Holiday House, 1993.

Gibbons, Gail. *Pirates: Robbers of the High Seas.* Boston: Little Brown & Co., 1993.

Shuter, Jane, ed. *Helen Williams and the French Revolution,* History Eyewitness. Austin, TX: Raintree/Steck, 1996.

Wallner, Alexandra. *Betsy Ross.* New York: Holiday House, 1998.

INDEX

PICTURE CREDITS

ABOUT THE AUTHOR ═══════

BRUCE and **BECKY DUROST FISH** are freelance writers and editors who have worked on more than 100 books for children and young adults. They have degrees in history and literature and live in the high desert of Central Oregon.

Senior Consulting Editor **ARTHUR M. SCHLESINGER, JR.** is the leading American historian of our time. He won the Pulitzer Prize for his book *The Age of Jackson* (1945), and again for *A Thousand Days* (1965). This chronicle of the Kennedy Administration also won a National Book Award. He has written many other books, including a multi-volume series, *The Age of Roosevelt.* Professor Schlesinger is the Albert Schweitzer Professor of the Humanities at the City University of New York, and has been involved in several other Chelsea House projects, including the Colonial Leaders series of biographies on the most prominent figures of early American history.